THE SHINING MATERIAL

THE SHINING MATERIAL

AISHA SASHA JOHN

BOOKTHUG   MMXI   TORONTO

FIRST EDITION

The production of this book was made possible through the generous assistance
of The Canada Council for The Arts and The Ontario Arts Council.

 Canada Council   Conseil des Arts
for the Arts   du Canada

 ONTARIO ARTS COUNCIL
CONSEIL DES ARTS DE L'ONTARIO

Printed in Canada.

Library and Archives Canada Cataloguing in Publication

John, Aisha Sasha
        The shining material / Aisha Sasha John.

Poems.
ISBN 978-1-897388-79-2

        I. Title.

PS8619.O444S55 2011   C811'.6   C2011-901536-6

to my Ma & Daddy

TABLE OF CONTENTS

SELF-PORTRAIT SELF-HUGGING 9

CAHIERS, JUILLET À AOÛT 2008 12

AND I'LL BE A BUTTON OF HARD BRIGHTNESS MOVING
ACROSS THE HORIZON 14

EVERYDAY ABANDON 18

SELF-PORTRAIT WITH YOU 19

CAHIERS, DÉCEMBRE 2008 À JANVIER 2009 20

SELF-PORTRAIT FERTILE 21

SELF-PORTRAIT FOG 23

SELF-PORTRAIT WASHING DISHES 24

CAHIERS, SEPTEMBRE À NOVEMBRE 2008 25

SELF-PORTRAIT CEMETERY 27

SELF-PORTRAIT OUTSIDE 28

SELF-PORTRAIT ENGLISH 30

SELF-PORTRAIT GRADE 12 31

CAHIERS, FÉVRIER À MAI 2009 32

SELF-PORTRAIT CHILD 34

POST-BAHIA 35

SELF-PORTRAIT HOUSED 37

SELF-PORTRAIT SUMMER 2004 39
CAHIERS, JANVIER À MAI 2010 40
SELF-PORTRAIT AS RAT 42
DON'T YOU KNOW YOU'RE WORTHY? 43
SELF-PORTRAIT A ~~HYPOCRITE~~ 44
SELF-PORTRAIT PORTRAIT 45
SELF-PORTRAIT AT A POETRY READING 46
INVOLVED 47
HAVE YOU EVER WATCHED TELEVISION? 48
CAHIERS, JUIN À SEPTEMBRE 2009 49
SELF-PORTRAIT WITH TRACEY EMIN'S TOWER DRAWINGS 50
SELF-PORTRAIT AT TRACEY EMIN'S MONOPRINTS 51
CAHIERS, OCTOBRE À DÉCEMBRE 2009 53
CELIA 54
SELF-PORTRAIT DANCING 56
WOULD LIKE TO WEEP 57
THE SHINING MATERIAL 58
THE SHINING MATERIAL II 60
SELF-PORTRAIT A READER 61

SELF-PORTRAIT SELF-HUGGING

elegance being a favourite escape
elegance itself always wanting
it felt true and that's elegance, grace
like a calm
wind I am
happy to know such elegance and
scared, maybe, to show all my elegance
how time didn't halt it.
over a season having passed
and I'm ripe here still with elegance
I'm ripe here still with elegance
and it isn't a lack of grace
that's got me
and I haven't anything to be short of
or flush-faced about
this all here bodaciously wetly
elegant. so elegant
I'm elegant now: not hiding, not
covering all the stuck want
it's elegant even to name it:
oh silk, feathers, clouds
blush and rub soft elegant smooth
all of his elegant slimness I hate him
I want him it's superior it's famous it's elegant
hating want what
waste

I'm still soft.

and what if he knew and he pushed hard
and what if he knew and he
scoffed and smirked and moved
elsewhere uncaring uncaring inelegant
what is left there to want he's in-
he's inelegant for days

and to resist makes the tension mountains, so
I'm valley elegant
I'm rolling green and billowing breezes
short flowers, lost petals: there's elegance to a small flower half-bare
its stem bent elegant and elegant it's okay it's fine
I won't end
up like her
I'm much more, modes more elegant
moving with gobs. dripping wet
grace.

he can't take that from me.

elegant he frustrates, switching
shit around
ignoring me inelegant, so

may I Lord please have some grace?

and if he's not there can I so elegant move unawkwardly
and if he is I'll drink the juice of that sight
mister, don't say anything please inelegant. don't be inelegant.

maybe, I still want you everyday.

well, yes.
and so
how to perform frost?

never.

that is so inelegant.
let any warm wind blow. let warmth go that's grace.

and what if I cry?

what if.

guess what you're a red-blood a human girl.
guess what. and so what.
you're a red-blood, a human woman and strong.
and the tears would be all elegant.

dede had warts
on his hands like roots.
warts on his feet like roots.
like bark, warts on his arm.
like bark, warts on his face on his
legs colonies of warts many inches long are his feet.
where are his hands?
heavy.
six inch warts of green-brown.
ten inch warts of green-brown.
dede whose dad makes him lunch is
in flesh like the roots of trees:
a strain of hpv.
she's gone.
dede all
tree
his hands
feet his
heavy
skin all root
his bark,
wart.

::

come girl I'll meet you and I'll take you in your hand
that's quite a something when you draw them back
and it's teeth teeth teeth teeth
your mouth looks full of cloud

    ::

And what? I don't know. And a bird: I don't
know. And his name? I don't know. I don't know.

AND I'LL BE A BUTTON OF HARD BRIGHTNESS MOVING ACROSS THE HORIZON

I never knew you so loose
edges
uncrisp
borders sky-sullied in barbados you showed incredible length

might I bathe
in you,
might I take your
fluff for sea?

a dress of you, cloud
brassiere
cloud skirt you
cool me

oh to reach
my hand and cloud, a scoop of you inside me
I'd beat
birds

cloud as a hairpiece

cloud in my exhale

my inhale pure sky

(the blue like piano jazz: dah. dah-dah dah.)

cloud in my nail whites

cut cloud for teeth

snot stuck hair to cheek

if you cut me I will bleed cloud

from above
a cloud is popcorn and wet towel rags

and the call
of cloud upon great bouncing trees
is the softest, charcoal shade

ask me anything and I'll tell you

this afternoon I will claw at the sky

catching clouds beneath my fingernails

wet breasts of sky

i'd like them at my face

EVERYDAY ABANDON

serious as
heated, free-
flowing glue
to the blare of a flute I would
having unbrushed brows and
a pilled brassiere
powerful my machines
coursing along a river with stiff, held-together
fingers

SELF-PORTRAIT WITH YOU

proving to ourselves we
know how to
feel good

you're on yonge street in
a grey velvet
track suit,
eyes the golden orbs
of a spiritual dog they
pour light into me,
a warm
pool of light that will nevertheless
cut   that's where want is rude.
          that want I fling,
snot-want, wet-on-the-wall
flicked want:
loss the square root of which is
raw
though when in want you're
sure for
lack knows itself
tremendous-
ly
well.
eyelashes,
how you love
to share your paint with cheek.

SELF-PORTRAIT FERTILE

So inwardly insistent
and moreover I couldn't distinguish any of your
machines

inasmuch as I am alien
ovaried bubbled and
possible.

How your
tendernesses were distinct from oily-fingered
instances, tell.

I also use:
an epistle for any confession
chickpea spread of
honey and apricot that is how
my breath smells
ovaried, possible
the air being all mine here.

Possible for it's certain that
once moonly they drop.

I lose them
I lost
got a raging want
a gully-ugly you-ward insistence.
Garishly embarrassing I hid it.

This isn't even to you;
your recency is how you're here, plainly
circumstance.

Without a you anyway it's I, with one still
I, rich
with all this
air.

SELF-PORTRAIT FOG

drunk in the brows, calling out clouds

for not hugging you

(back) face slathered in dew

damp-breathed

SELF-PORTRAIT WASHING DISHES

pumping a hard water stream
to clear my inner fist of its suds

trees to say tree is reduction those are just leafy upstanding
beasts

::

Because I can't think without record.

::

I think you want disaster that will leave no scar
except story.
I think you want order—
for the life to match what you've read about.
I think you want to know
and you can't know
and you don't know
yet you must live—
you have to move, going
through it what is right
you want what is
smart you want
you want certainty.

well, too bad.

honey brown panther, long waist
like hot bread

      ::

When for
I to see yuh again
if in case I love yuh?

      ::

I prefer a mattress
covered in a ball of myself
gasping.

SELF-PORTRAIT CEMETERY

There was no precedent
just a headache, despair, three
cans of Asahi plastic-bagged and
there they were:
most punched into the earth like
square stud earrings,
the rest pushed out, erect,
fake flowers at their base the most
colourful pubic hair.
One grave said Lagos, Nigeria so I stood
by it clasping the beer with the full stretch
of my hand.

I was the only live body around.

SELF-PORTRAIT OUTSIDE

i might know exile but it would cease if i moved,
chose to walk other streets, another land
and to lose—
mouth swollen
heavy with
another's tongue.
if i changed places it would be that i am a visitor
a traveller,
moving

if one's frame of reference is home, exile

if young coquitlam firs, six a.m. coyotes—   exile

my mother phoning me about a bear cub at her garbage
like i know lolita is in the basement there—
what other books didn't i begin?
it's their home and i stank it, i came and i left and

bled, mostly: exile. he said, he said he would call the cops if i came back;
he'd like the key. i haven't and i won't give it back all over my face is his
mother and exile that would make him me. hello, father. you are all over
everything. that bump you grew at your crown—have it removed. i too
have one; i'm only you and you take yourself too seriously. what i want
is a poke at irreverence. i bought a burrito today and the man who sold
it to me had pee wee herman inked on his arm and "burrito fuck yeah"
lapping the fat of his left back and i envied him. daddy, i'm outside/
here/toronto looking for a land because you've given me this very

exquisite rich quiet machine, this gift how many are (i am) exiled? i am;
it is outside it is possible; it has made me fertile ravenous lost shining.
daddy? daddy, it's me aisha. remove the bump on your head: it makes
you look crazy. and get your shit out my room. i want to come back. i'll
be quiet about all your wrongnesses. just kidding. i'll never quiet. i'm
relentless. i'm you. yeah, right: i'm better. kidding. lose the bump.

SELF-PORTRAIT ENGLISH

Try Tylenol, triathlete: Tylenol.

Try chess, tri-cities (Co-

quitlam, Poco, Port Moody,

Maple Ridge, Iraq). The

calabash went bracalack brugodung—it fell.

Cornucopia? Cup?

Casket? Consolation?

You think you know so much, you don't know shit,

big-lettered, big belly

butter-balled, baked

unidentified automaton.

The beech fell flat. It died.

Slides, swings. Bush, Kate. Barack Obama

bannock cooked fresh by

Temesgen.

Do your homework. Now.

Wait,

Youse my fada or suh-in? You got a *problem*, my man?

SELF-PORTRAIT GRADE 12

ck one, bus tickets, some mother's car, frozen orange juice crystals
spooned into the slim neck of a vodka bottle, bomb scar
shiny, taut on the shoulder of one boy
another boy's
penthouse
inside of which I
was a tourist, passing

and these boys aren't full even: stuttering, wet, timid
with control.
and these boys strum, nod, elasticate, convince,
bury, these boys drum kits in their nose hairs
freshly beaten asses waving to a tender vancouver night from
a white convertible, expletives fingered in dust, okay?
the boys sat treasuring, malignant, filing cabinets full
one year younger
one lap around the block, me "holding" their cigarettes
a drag is three, buzzed from one drag, thanks you can
have it back

grace it drips from our thighs let us
catch it
and grace it hangs from our chest no we need not
contain it no, grace

::

you could say i'm uninterested in categories but that's what you
would say. i say why tell the raccoon his back is too arched.
should he wear a brace now?

::

Returning after the lunch bell
teeth full of a soft
metal alloy.
The fat that knew our cheeks.
Thresheld.
Transparent.
Teen-aged
women so white of
eyes. Smell our breath.

This is—what is?—natural.
This is—what is?—just.
This is—what is?—uncommon.

     ::

That is

                     breasts falling into a palm

what soft means

     ::

I think it could hold. I think I have the thick legs of patience.

and I didn't think all the salmon would
wither.

surrendering what could have been a famous
first time.

what I have is abundance do you want it.
lacking control
inaugural
do you want
it?

SELF-PORTRAIT CHILD

the buzz of fluorescent lights
needy industrial succinct how
uncinnamon this Sunday evening
away hungry as
boiling water let me
my Ma:
our laughter the roar of a
hot-oiled pan at cut
onion

POST-BAHIA

this blazing
stolid snow she
provides this city
I hate
inasmuch as she imprisons me with
all of her resources:
love.
hands left in warm water will be sodden
and Toronto has wrinkled my hands
Toronto has made soggy my hands

and the last time I tried to get true I merely lied to you
that was the cloth I was interested in clothing myself in
in covering my head with that was the hood that was the shawl that
was the kind of sunlight for which one didn't want shade and the sea water
that bettered my swath of Dominican
madras in a
traditional colour and traditional pattern: a traditional cloth.

the sound of internet café typing plus the rumble
of an air conditioning portal the moment before
I was going to get my ignorance ripped from me so I cradled it
and shutting my eyes it fell
out of my mouth like
sin does
like judgement and smallness
and gaping all I was was a vessel, a wanting, and the new sight
rushed into my

mouth
the new sight just poured into my mouth, so when
I turned around swiftly it fell out
and so did a bunch of
other things like
certainty and quiet
leaving
the loud roar of a confusion
blasting confusion

discovering
it was clairvoyance that lied
that held its science over and left:
surprise
in the hammock one moment, leisurely as the sizzle of
canned cola, and in the next, ankle banged skin hanging
cowering behind the bed,
a shot a pause two more.
cocooned, then I remembered where I was.
tell me please what exactly all of it means:
all of that thereness: conspicuous, unopposite, percussive, better?
and here, this
dull and perfect metaphor
masking, toxic and white, this hot and shit-strewn
snow

SELF-PORTRAIT HOUSED

In the beginning we looked to her place and we shut our mind to
her place because there were noises.
Chopin playing lightly and he's not for drowning. And she stomps and she
stomps and
what is our interest in her place? We wonder about
menses, what tool she uses to
sop it
is she, is she human in all
respects, i.e. really does she release and wipe, gas and
stool? She's so

Yeah? I have the keys to her place twelve days let's
enquire. I believe I know her credit limit. It's laughable.
What she could do more with is control and her place, her
place betrays her. Three pairs of mittens not one of them
matching not one.
I've been to her place a couple of times a few times, crumb
on the water glass. That's all. That was all she had to
drink and I had to ask. Oh and Campari but who
wants that? Cheap
rent at her place
I, I wouldn't
mind that I pay oh, I don't even want to tell you what I pay
terrible. It's terrible.
She hasn't called since
she's left
it's been oh I don't I

have to say the bathroom's huge and the lighting is very
tasteful. One of the lamps bought with a gift certificate I gave
her so basically I bought
I bought it for her, basically. She could use some
plants.

SELF-PORTRAIT SUMMER 2004

Sweat beneath
my breasts feet raw
with the rub of bad sandals,
searing, I wanted
cool mist, a body-
length box, a lid.
In that photo my beauty is terrible.
Our beauty—we were three:
Jake, Aisha, Badi.
My eyebrows as thin as
rock salt. The base of your thumb, a drumstick.
His dusty, perfect,
quiet feet. Terrible,
terrible, terrible.

and if you move forward not caring about the
tidy, the sushi roll
cleanly
I am so fucking messy
and look at my mouth.

     ::

Titties as cold as force. Swinging titties conical
you how
light you felt in your skin alone was
HOLY

     ::

when you'd burst outside of all you'd eaten and barfing on the floor held
a fizzed glass of very cold liquid to your right temple and
sang a dorothy danbridge song to create romance out of abjection.
going to wikipedia to learn about elephants and narcissistic personality disorder.
going to wikipedia to find links for porn stars and modernist poetry.

I went to Britannia Community Centre Summer Day Camp for three years as a kid. We would go to Stanley Park, go to the beaches, Second Beach, and bring home little grey crabs and sand in styrofoam cups. The cups stank like the sea and we would smell them on the bus home because they stank and the crabs would die and we'd get back to the gym, cups stinking of sea and death. Once I insulted another kid, a girl, and one of the junior counsellors told me I had no right saying what I'd said 'cause I was black and ugly and I had big ugly lips. And I remember thinking, *my lips aren't even that big.*

::

because I want to piss into someone's eye and give him
reason to be passionate.

and for fuck's sake.

because you're inside you don't see how
small the aesthetic is
and where is anything radical or forward
hello?
hello?

SELF-PORTRAIT AS RAT

we knew machines.
we had them we ran them.
our lives they led them we were
machines the name of which is
wage.
I ate a lot of bacon
masks shit I ate both daily.
so frequently
demeaned there I lost several natural competencies: grace, subjecthood,
retort.
high-priced shoes the sight of them at my footrest soothed me.
one year passed my machine
was assessed:
you show too much natural breast:
finally, I died. good
afternoon human
resources
may I help you?

DON'T YOU KNOW YOU'RE WORTHY?

so I choked on balls of cotton

so I was dry in the mouth

so I spoke through my eyes unsuccessfully

so I let my hands speak and they were loud

though everything I said was a moan

SELF-PORTRAIT A ~~HYPOCRITE~~

my
embarrassed
my
six thousand dollars my
mouth:
lingual braces.
I keep my premolars in an orange pill bottle.
they yanked
four whole to
make space
pull my buck teeth back

where they belong.

orthodontist
saying my mouth not
unusual, not unAfrican and I know, I
replied, *Fix it.*   Fix it.
my mouth
projects forward
still it
and I
of course,
almost don't hate it.
every day

I would do it again.

SELF-PORTRAIT PORTRAIT

the
violence   of
self-   definition

SELF-PORTRAIT AT A POETRY READING

How did I not see it before their
voracity? These writers are bush
wolves hungry in their meekness, hungry are they
nervous. No wonder they hate me
soft as I am and open about
my arrogance.

INVOLVED

all day long
all traces were told again today I know
when I told you, you
you
you
you
you
relentless that's it's again you
who and
very very you
you're calling
I call it colonize
you
you
you
focused to the point of
blur

I might be it you or together we are
because that's our shared goal:
yourself
let's know about you more and more
it's you you
you
again you
ten out of ten you
I'm looking, I'm looking

HAVE YOU EVER WATCHED TELEVISION?

Let me touch your hair feel your titties. What do you have to tell?
What do you have to tell—is it seedy?
Okay, fine.
How about every day I say you're dumb and ugly
and you agree and try to erase yourself?

How about you bleed from every instance? When you're dying I can feel
you and I like that.
Be Haiti.

CAHIERS, JUIN À SEPTEMBRE 2009

There's a man with a striped shirt.
There's a man with a striped shirt, another man.
There is a woman with a polka dot blouse.
Cashew pieces this may contain nuts.
This is the first time
I've seen you flat and dry and digital.
There is an insurrection digital fingers.
There is a man in a striped shirt shivering.
There is a dotted-bloused woman strengthening her
upper lower back.

::

they look well they look awfully soft.

::

should I
spend on a bus ticket to go home to go to metro to get food to be fed
to know strength to have resolve to work to go on to go go to charge
through to sit basking to open out to in-no-vate to best to make it money
to buy to buy a bag of apple chips pork chops yogurt organic eggs and
milk?

and bananas?

SELF-PORTRAIT WITH TRACEY EMIN'S TOWER DRAWINGS

tower drawing 4

Sometimes a woman is an ant
eater is a mole, has paws, prays at a
crystalline tower.

tower drawing 7

Is she blowing smoke?
(Am I? Do you?)

A mirage of a big-boobied lady?

Is she led by string?
Is she leashed by
loops of
dark blue drool?

tower drawing 3

It's perfect
the length of the human arm.
Today my
pussy is a butterfly.

tower drawing 27

A belly pregnant is so perfect it must stop.

SELF-PORTRAIT AT TRACEY EMIN'S MONOPRINTS

why all the money millions they pay some soft fools for
it is the worst kind of desire
the eye infinitely outside
and the page said come, so I came

it is the worst kind of desire
to look at tracey emin's monoprints I feel both her and extremely lonely
and the page said come, so I came
I came

to look at tracey emin's monoprints I feel both her and extremely lonely
looking—it doesn't join; it grazes
I came
I am talking about art here

looking—it doesn't join; it grazes
it is the worst kind of desire
I am talking about art here
it does me and I stand there

it is the worst kind of desire
I let it I like that
I am talking about art here
it does me and I stand there

I let it I like that
I could just look at them everyday
it does me and I stand there
I would look at them everyday let me

I could just look at them everyday
everyday
I would look at them everyday let me
every perfect day

when the men called you elephant what did you lie there open maggots
upon the rabbit's genitalia, something in its ear made it think
the world a ride, upside down
and it dragged itself shitting indiscriminately

::

what about the elephants. what's said of an elephant?
ass. climb. in. fall:
all of the elephant insides. oh
take my nose and
blow hard

::

I don't know if elephant

I don't know is what I mean to say if elephant meat is the future
and you said you were done with self-address

CELIA

immediate portable
eternal
very very cheap
fast
thought being good
is
fire
how much of it do you stock?
is long
I would have some
coffee coffee
and I would take it with cream
and I would have in it honey
and I would drink it
with slow
and I would thence wolf food with grace
and I would aftersip some water
and I would return to the beast and prattle
a sinner
I wrote and in that's light
lava
a cartonful
each tap of the broom singing to me
celia
celia
celia
that isn't my name but said it's my song
the soft of the ce and lia, what is more feminine

endings in ah stand open
and last
the cilia
you cost so many times
I'll crisp up to leave you tenderly
you perfect shawl
you
you tenderoni you
you delicious mistake you
you
shining
this place
tamer than shorn hair

SELF-PORTRAIT DANCING

soft

generous

blistering

ripe sky. a slate-coloured sea. red slits smiling along a fat cracked steaming river. baby goats, baby otters, baby walruses crying. dry-eyed sea turtles mating—sea turtles laying wet, white eggs. there are times when I'd rather the sleep not stop. animal, glistening, arrogant, roaring, wet, little white eggs.

WOULD LIKE TO WEEP

also, I wanted to see about being holy
and then my right hand again
first my left hand then
God is in my neck and
God is in my neck
I can feel her in my neck
I clapped
I've seen God come from her mouth
if I pull hard enough I can join her
if I take each hand and run it down the front of my neck
it's like He and I are holding hands
let's be spiritual, I said to my friend
my right hand
she has a giant song
then my left hand

THE SHINING MATERIAL

call: I would like to hold your hands.

response: The Shining Material. The Shining Material.

call: Tell me where we can go
               to be alone and have some kind of communion.

response: The Shining Material. The Shining Material.

call: I would like to hold your hands.

response: The Shining Material. The Shining Material.

call: You breathe and I
               sing an original song and you cry and I breathe and
               speak an original language and you move and, and
               and—

response: The Shining Material. The Shining Material.

call: Take a small fruit and swallow its skin and seed and
               take a small fruit and bleed
               the juice of it on my calf to know.

response: The Shining Material. The Shining Material.

call: On your own calf
               take a small fruit and bleed the juice of it to know
               something empirically.

response: The Shining Material. The Shining Material.

call: Yes, to feel.

response: The Shining Material. The Shining Material.

call: Yes, to feel.

response: The Shining Material. The Shining Material.

call: I would like to hold your hands.

response: The Shining Material. The Shining Material.

call: Hold my hand and I'll hum and your
movement might get patterned:
arms wide, exalt, wrists strong, hurrah,
begin: shining, shining
us us us   onto, at, for, within,
shining,
mouth out,
shining,
boom for real,
the beauty, the beauty—it's ours, it is ours.

response: The Shining Material. The Shining Material.

call: I would like to hold your hand.

THE SHINING MATERIAL II

Somebody told me that I Should.
Somebody told me that I Should.
And I said,

No.

SELF-PORTRAIT A READER

all the day does is change me.

ACKNOWLEDGEMENTS

I'd like to acknowledge the Ontario Arts Council for support received through the Writers' Reserve Program. Thanks also to the editors/publishers who recommended the work.

Thanks to the editors of the following publications for publishing earlier versions of some of these poems: *The Capilano Review, Dear Sir, Existere,* and *White Wall Review.*

Ma—Thank you for everything.

Daddy—Thanks for everything, too.

Mayko—Thank you.

Andrea—Thank you.

Nadia—Thank you.

Hesper—Thank you.

Fana—Thank you.

Dionne—Thank you.

Lisa—Thank you.

Jay—Thank you.

Miss Bailey, Alison Sullings, Deborah Knott, Rosemary Sullivan—Thank you.

COLOPHON

Manufactured in an edition of 500 copies in the spring of 2011 by BookThug. Distributed in Canada by the Literary Press Group: www.lpg.ca. Distributed in the United States by Small Press Distribution: www.spdbooks.org.
Shop on-line at www.bookthug.ca.

BOOK
PRODUCTION
WAR ECONOMY
STANDARD

Type + design by Jay MillAr